Fred Tozer's

NEWTON ABBOT

Album

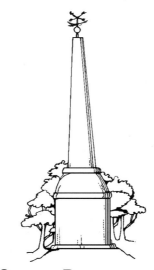

OBELISK PUBLICATIONS

Other Books in this Series

Other Obelisk Publications

First Published in 1993 by Obelisk Publications
2 Church Hill, Pinhoe, Exeter, Devon
Designed by Chips and Sally Barber
Typeset by Sally Barber
Printed in Great Britain by
Sprint Print Co Ltd, Okehampton Place, Exeter

For further details of these or any of our extensive Devon titles, please contact us at 2 Church Hill, Pinhoe, Exeter, EX4 9ER, Tel: (0392) 468556.

ISBN: 0 946651 73 6

THE TOWER, NEWTON ABBOT.

Whenever Newton Abbot is depicted in a single photograph this view is the one that is normally chosen. St. Leonard's Tower is shown here as it looked in 1905 when traffic was virtually non-existent.

Courtney St, Newton Abbot.

On these two pages we have two similar views of Courtenay St. Apart from the spelling, on the postcard, can you spot the major difference between the two scenes?

The Weslyan Chapel, in this picture, has a spire but in the opposite scene it is missing! It was removed about 1926 when it was discovered that the weather vane was leaning at a dangerous angle. Closer inspection revealed that the timber spire itself was in need of replacement but funds were not available. Later the building was sold to Woolworth's who demolished it. Today it is the site of W. H. Smith, where you might have bought this book!

COURTENAY ST NEWTON ABBOT. 18808.

Newton has a long tradition of being a market town drawing in people and products from a wide area of South Devon and Dartmoor. Here we see the Uren sisters with their fruit barrel in Courtenay Street. Later they progressed to having a market stall selling similar produce for many years.

This splendid photograph, taken in the days of horse-drawn traffic, shows The Globe on the corner of Courtenay St. The original fire station was nearby and whenever the service was called upon, the wagon was brought into Courtenay St, as there was more room there to attach the horses to the wagon shafts. On one occasion when there was a fire in nearby Bank St, the boy charged with the task of holding the horses let go when one reared and they escaped up the road! The firemen had to pull the appliance to the scene of the fire, which was well alight, before they started tackling it.

The hustle and bustle of Newton's livestock market has always attracted crowds. Although it has stayed in a similar location there have been changes down the years and these next pages illustrate that. This view dates back to about 1910.

Again we have two similar views but with several years between them. The vehicles are a give away in showing that the photo on this page is the older of the two.

The cars are much more modern and there are more buildings in the middle distance but it has all changed a lot more since then!

(Opposite) Whilst the multi-storey car park was being built the market had to move temporarily and function in cramped conditions.

The photograph above was taken before the modernisation of Market Walk, now the Market Precinct.

QUEEN STREET, NEWTON ABBOT.

Here are two views of Queen St in an age when traffic, what little there was, flowed in both directions. The most prominent building is The Congregational Church, still a landmark for miles around. However when it opened, in April 1876, it did not possess a spire. This was added in 1910!

QUEEN ST NEWTON ABBOT. 18811.

Older Newtonians will recall the name of Bibbings, the pharmaceutical chemist, whose premises are shown on the right hand side of the picture.

49711. Queen Street, Newton Abbot.

The Commercial Hotel stood at the end of Queen St. Many years ago the hotel kept its own horse-drawn carriages for picking up its customers from the railway station and for carrying people on other routes. The hotel was demolished to make way for Pearl Assurance House now housing the Brittanic Building Society and Ivor Doble, the jewellers.

THE STATION, NEWTON ABBOT.

Newton's railway station was an important one. At its peak it had many engine sheds and extensive sidings. Railway routes converged on the town from various directions and many a passenger has spent time waiting for a change of train on one of the long, impressive platforms.

These two photographs are linked. The beautiful old oak tree was felled and the money raised was used towards the cost of the war memorial on the opposite page.

A large crowd gathered, in 1922, for the unveiling ceremony of the memorial to the dead of The Great War.

Courtenay Park, Newton Abbot.

Courtenay Park has long been a favourite place for Newtonians with its wide open spaces, its strategically located benches and in the past its bandstand and performing bands.

Newton Abbot, Courtenay Park, Bowling Green.

Another attraction is the bowling green, seen here long before the days of fine playing surfaces. The standard dress for playing this game seemed to be suits then!

Forde House has been many things to many people! Built in the shape of the letter E, this house was built for Sir Richard Reynell. In 1625 it entertained two illustrious guests, the Duke of Buckingham and Charles I.

Newton Abbott.

Ford House

When William of Orange breezed through, he also stayed here. The people of Newton have always been proud that he made an important proclamation in the town. Forde House has been a hotel and an antique salesroom before being bought by the local authority. The pond was filled in much to the disappointment of many locals! Spot the spelling mistake in the picture?

SHALDON AND ST. MARY CHURCH ROADS, NEWTON ABBOT.

201904. J.V.

Note – just one car! This view should be instantly recognisable to the thousands of motorists who go up or down here every day. This photograph, taken about 1927, shows a motor car heading up the hill towards Shaldon. Just above it, on the right, is a large house where the present turning right towards St Marychurch is executed. The little stretch of road to the right of the sign is now a cul-de-sac.

Penn Inn is not far from Forde House and the area around it has seen more change since the last war than many places in the district. Here we have the 'family boating lake', which is shown in pristine condition shortly after its opening. Construction took twelve months – 1 July 1936 to 1 July 1937! In its life, which amounted to less than half a century, it gave many children (and quite a few adults!) much pleasure.

SWIMMING POOL. NEWTON ABBOT. 20,119.

These swimming pool pictures will also revive happy memories for those who spent warm summer days at the outdoor pool.

THE SWIMMING POOL, NEWTON ABBOT

Plymco's supermarket now fills the site where Newtonians splashed about in blissful ignorance of what was to happen here in later years.

This is the farthest that we get away from Newton on this side of the town. These houses at Kingskerswell Road, Decoy were then known as Greenbank Terrace, and had not been here all that long when this photo was taken. Apart from a handful of people the street is deserted, not even a single animal availing itself of the drinking trough that stood here at the time.

This fine photograph is of Bank St where the Mitre Bookshop is now located on the right hand side. The road was originally called Bridge St but when the bridge disappeared and a number of banks appeared it changed name. Today it has no banks!

On these two pages we have another pair of similar views, this time of Wolborough St, once the location of several pubs. In this photo the gable end on the extreme right is that of The Turk's Head. Next to it was The Royal Oak and beside that was The Half Moon.

This photograph looks to the left of its partner on the opposite page and shows the demolition of the building beside the general stores. The pubs, except for The Turks Head, were also demolished to make way for Newfoundland Way.

The other side of Wolborough St has also witnessed considerable change. Here buildings have been demolished to create space for what is now Wolborough St car park.

Newton Abbot town centre lies in the path and influence of the River Lemon. This humble watercourse starts its life in a mire close to Haytor Rocks, a landmark clearly visible from Newton's high spots. Throughout the years, whenever there has been heavy and prolonged rainfall, this river has hurtled down from the moors to inflict misery and discomfort on the low-lying parts of the town.

Scenes like this one have regularly appeared in the local press and the Lemon, despite its lack of stature, has been given much attention. Hopefully schemes upstream have reduced its capability to inundate the town centre like this. This (and the picture on the next page) was taken in 1938 when 4.87 inches of rainfall, well over a normal average month's worth fell in ten hours. The storm that yielded this downpour, at the time, had been the worst in living memory. It began at 3.00 a.m. and heralded a night of terror for residents and shopkeepers alike.

This is Little Venice in Bank St on Thursday, 3 August 1938! The Lemon, in its bid to squeeze through Newton, overspilled its banks in spectacular fashion. People can be spied trudging along the pavement by the Passmore-Edwards Library at the end of the street.

Ogwell Mill, Newton Abbot.

The river that caused so much anguish and despair also was of great use to man at times and the Lemon between its source and its confluence with the Teign had many mills. This was Ogwell Mill shown here as an idyllic scene, which painters and photographers travelled long distances to capture, with its overshot waterwheel and quaint stone buildings. At one time it is believed to have been used as a monastery, an ideal rural retreat. The last milling family to live there were called Loder and emigrated to America in 1909. It then became a tea room, selling the best cream teas in the district, up to the First World War. However an inspection after the war revealed that the building was unsafe. A storm demolished part of the building and it was abandoned to the mercy of scavengers and the elements.

33

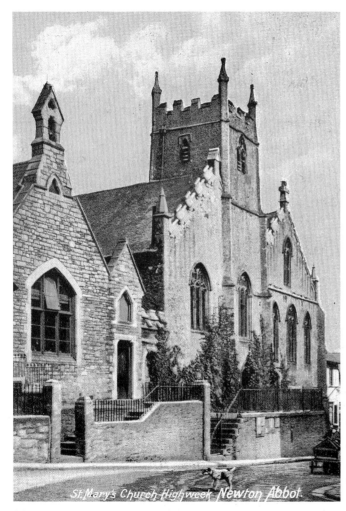

St. Mary's Church Highweek Newton Abbot.

Highweek St is slightly higher ground and the church of St Mary's was built on solid ground safe from any possible inundation. Today it has been 'converted' into residential flats.

(opposite) This picture shows us much more of Highweek St. Many of the buildings on the near left side of the photo have been demolished. Just beyond the telephone box, on the left, was Fields and Son, a dairy, and next to that was the Priest House. When this building was demolished all the stonework was carefully numbered so that, at some time, it could be reconstructed on another site. Alas this never materialised and the only memory lies in photographs like this. At the top of the road was a fork: left lead to Highweek and Ashburton whilst the right turn was Exeter Road towards Bovey Tracey. Where the garage is on the right is now the new entrance to Halcyon Road.

Coombes Head Road, Highweek Road.

It is always surprising to see some views as picture postcards and these two of 'Highweek Road' are surprise choices. Bisected by Ashburton Road, it is now a cul-de-sac. The houses on the left have been clad in bricks making them much smarter and better insulated.

Broadlands P.O., Highweek Road.

Broadlands Post Office, as the building was then, was not averse to advertising and placed signs wherever they could. Now it is a confectionery shop.

The streets were not exactly packed for the royal visit of The Duke and Duchess of York. The Duke is shown here in Queen Street near the Congregational Church (now solicitors' offices) acknowledging the cheers of the spectators lining the pavement. The photographer had a perfect view of the proceedings.

Jimmy Steere is stood in the doorway to his shop, dressed in his soldier's uniform. He was a talented man who, in peace time, would entertain with his one man band show. His versatility was amply displayed in the way that he supplemented the income from his shop by doubling up as a chimney sweep. However, if he ever cleaned in a house that had a piano, he couldn't resist the temptation to tinkle on the ivories. This meant that after he'd finished it was impossible to tell the white notes from the black!

A.C. Bulpin were the pioneers of petrol-driven tractors in Newton Abbot. Here an excited assembly paraded the first one to be seen in the town. To test its strength it repeatedly circumnavigated the Market buildings pulling Vicary's steam wagon (driven by Ned Hill). Mr Bulpin Junior is shown here driving the tractor whilst the man in the trilby hat is A.C. Bulpin Senior. Others in the picture include Bill Stidwell in the white peaked cap and Frank White on the bicycle.

After the trial was successfully completed the crews and spectators posed for one more picture. Someone else is now ensconced in the driving seat for this 1924 photograph.

The "Newtonian" Off for the Moors.

J.W.S.3211

Dartmoor has always been a favourite destination for the good folk of Newton, some of the most scenic spots being within easy striking distance. "The Newtonian" is shown here outside the railway station ready to convey a party up to the moors, probably to Becky Falls or to some of the many tors of the eastern moor.

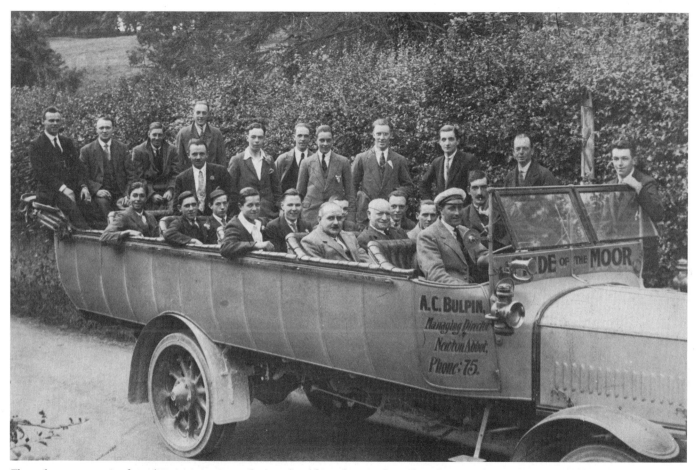

The railway companies forged routes to towns on the moorland fringe but people preferred to get to the parts trains couldn't reach. A C. Bulpin's "Pride of the Moor", which could be hired by telephoning Newton Abbot 75, is featured in the next few pages. Amongst the throng are Stidwell, the driver, Fred Ash, Les Cane, Alex Albrighton, Fred Hales, Tom Perkins and Dave Edge.

Headwear seems the order of the day for this outing. 'The Pride of the Moor', again with Mr Stidwell in relaxed pose, gets ready to go off on almost traffic-free roads (what bliss!) and has paused for posterity outside Newton Abbot's Co-op Store in Courtenay Street.

The last picture of this celebrated charabanc shows a smiling contingent, unusual in photos like this when people usually look stern! Hopefully the suspension was in order as the lady in the back was about to give it a good road test!

Although this collection is mainly of street scenes and views, it should be of interest to long-established locals to see a few pictures of people – even though they have probably passed on. This grand bunch of fellows used their spare time and their talents to entertain audiences in the area. The Buff Blues Harmonica Band included my uncle, Edgar Rundle; I still possess the silky blue costume that he wore in this photo! The man below the name of the band was Stan Renton.

This was the cast of a French titled production: Les Cloches de Caineville *that was staged at* The Alexandra Theatre *on 20, 21 and 22 April 1922 by the Newton Abbot Operatic and Dramatic Society.*

We end with this picture taken in Queen St from the corner by The Courtenay Arms looking towards The Drum Clock. On the right is Madge Mellor's Restaurant where many Newtonians dined over a span of many years.

The names, places and faces continue to change but I hope you have enjoyed this nostalgic look at Newton Abbot of yesteryear.

Many of these pictures have been collected whilst I have gone about my daily task as a dustbin man. So, if you have any pictures you don't want, please let me know, and I will give them a good home...